SACRA... P9-CKK-402

828 I Street
Sacramento, CA 95814
05/20

Foundation

THIS BOOK WAS DONATED BY
The Sacramento Public Library Foundation
Books and Materials Endowment

The Sacramento Public Library gratefully acknowledges this
contribution to support and improve Library services in the community.

SACRAMENTO PUBLIC LIBRARY

WORLD LEADERS

NARENDRA MODI
PRIME MINISTER OF INDIA

by Alexis Burling

FOCUS READERS

www.focusreaders.com

Copyright © 2019 by Focus Readers, Lake Elmo, MN 55042. All rights reserved. No part of this book may be reproduced or utilized in any form or by any means without written permission from the publisher.

Focus Readers is distributed by North Star Editions:
sales@northstareditions.com | 888-417-0195

Produced for Focus Readers by Red Line Editorial.

Content Consultant: Susan Ostermann, Assistant Professor of Global Affairs, University of Notre Dame

Photographs ©: Narayan Maharjan/NurPhoto/Sipa USA/AP Images, cover, 1; arindambanerjee/Shutterstock Images, 4–5; nisargmediaproductions/Shutterstock Images, 7, 35; AravindTeki/iStockphoto, 8; kjohansen/iStockphoto, 10–11; Rainer Lesniewski/Shutterstock Images, 12, 26; Globe Turner/Shutterstock Images, 15; Max Nash/AP Images, 16–17; traveler1116/iStockphoto, 19; AP Images, 20, 22–23, 28–29, 43; Dazzlefleck/Shutterstock Images, 25; Ajit Kumar/AP Images, 31; Raj K Raj/Hindustan Times/Newscom, 32–33; Drop of Light/Shutterstock Images, 36; Manish Swarup/AP Images, 39; Channi Anand/AP Images, 40–41; Subhankar Chakraborty/Hindustan Times/Sipa USA/Newscom, 45

Library of Congress Cataloging-in-Publication Data
Library of Congress Cataloging-in-Publication Data is available on the Library of Congress website.

ISBN
978-1-64185-363-7 (hardcover)
978-1-64185-421-4 (paperback)
978-1-64185-537-2 (ebook pdf)
978-1-64185-479-5 (hosted ebook)

Printed in the United States of America
Mankato, MN
October, 2018

ABOUT THE AUTHOR

Alexis Burling has written dozens of articles and more than 20 books for young readers on a variety of topics. Though she hasn't yet traveled to India, she hopes to visit the majestic Taj Mahal in Uttar Pradesh someday soon.

TABLE OF CONTENTS

CHAPTER 1
A Historic Victory 5

CHAPTER 2
Humble Beginnings 11

COUNTRY PROFILE
Focus on India 14

CHAPTER 3
An Early Activist 17

CHAPTER 4
Entering Politics 23

CHAPTER 5
Crisis and Controversy 29

CHAPTER 6
Becoming Prime Minister 33

PERSON OF IMPACT
Focus on Arun Jaitley 38

CHAPTER 7
Challenges Ahead 41

Focus on Narendra Modi • 46
Glossary • 47
To Learn More • 48
Index • 48

A HISTORIC VICTORY

May 16, 2014, was a big day for India. The country was about to hold the largest democratic election in history. Nearly 814 million people were eligible to vote. The election would determine which political party would control India's government. The Congress Party had been in power for most years since India's first election in 1951. However, voters were growing unhappy with the way this party was running the country.

The Congress Party is one of India's two major political parties.

Inflation and inequality had been rising for years. Instead of solving these problems, the government had become corrupt. People were ready for a change.

Many Indians looked to Narendra Modi to make that change. Modi led the Bharatiya Janata Party (BJP). Unlike the Congress Party, which kept religious beliefs separate from government matters, the BJP was actively pro-Hindu. And in India, pro-Hindu often meant anti-Muslim. Although India has no official religion, more than 80 percent of Indians are Hindu. Approximately 14 percent are Muslim. Members of these two

> **THINK ABOUT IT**

Do you support combining religion and government? Or do you think they should be kept separate? Why?

▲ Narendra Modi waves to voters and wears a lotus flower, the symbol of the Bharatiya Janata Party (BJP).

religions have clashed several times throughout the country's history. Other religions in India include Buddhism, Christianity, Jainism, Judaism, and Sikhism.

During his **campaign**, Modi focused on solving problems people faced. He promised to create millions of jobs. He planned to invest money in energy, roads, and railroads. In addition, he called for more government accountability.

▲ Both houses of India's Parliament meet in the Sansad Bhavan, or Parliament House, in New Delhi.

India has a parliamentary form of government. The president is the official head of state. But that job is mostly symbolic. Parliament creates the laws and runs the government. India's Parliament has two houses. The upper house is called the Rajya Sabha, or the Council of States. Members of this house are chosen by each state's legislature. They are not elected by voters. But voters do elect the members of their state's legislature.

The lower house is the Lok Sabha, or the House of the People. Voters elect its members directly.

To form a government on its own, a political party must win at least 272 of this house's 543 seats. Otherwise, parties must join together to form a coalition. When a party or coalition has a majority, its members vote to select the prime minister. This person leads India's government. Like other members of Parliament (MPs), the prime minister serves a five-year term.

In India, political parties typically announce their candidate for prime minister before the election. So, even though voters don't directly vote for the prime minister, they usually know who will be elected if one party wins.

In 2014, the BJP won 282 seats in the Lok Sabha. For the first time in 30 years, a single party had won a clear majority. Modi became India's new prime minister. The BJP leader had come a long way from his humble roots.

CHAPTER 2

HUMBLE BEGINNINGS

Narendra Modi was born on September 17, 1950. He grew up in a small town in the western state of Gujarat. His father was a street merchant. His mother took care of Narendra and his five siblings.

In India, society is divided into social ranks called castes. Each person is born into a caste, and there are not many ways to change it. The Modis were part of a lower caste called Ghanchi.

Gujarat, the Indian state where Modi grew up, is located along the country's western coast.

They lived in a tiny, single-story house. To make money, Narendra and his two older brothers helped their father run a stall that sold tea. The

➤ INDIA'S STATES AND TERRITORIES

India consists of 29 states and 7 union territories.

Modis practiced the Hindu religion. But Narendra also had many Muslim friends.

Narendra became interested in politics at a young age. By age 10, he had joined the Akhil Bharatiya Vidyarthi Parishad (ABVP). This group was the student wing of the Rashtriya Swayamsevak Sangh (RSS). The RSS is an organization that seeks to give Hindus political influence. Narendra attended classes and lectures to learn about the RSS. This training introduced him to ideas that would shape his political career.

Narendra began learning about Hindu nationalism. Of India's many religious groups, Hindus are the largest. Some people, such as RSS members, saw India as a Hindu nation. They believed India should have one culture, based on Hindu traditions and values. They wanted the country's government to reflect this view.

FOCUS ON

INDIA

From 1858 to 1947, India was a British **colony**. Then the colony was divided to form two independent countries. One was the Republic of India. The other was the Islamic Republic of Pakistan, which was later split into Pakistan and Bangladesh. A disputed territory called Kashmir separated India and Pakistan. The two countries still fight for control of this territory. Most people who live there are Muslim.

Today, India is the largest democracy in the world. In 2018, more than 1.3 billion people lived in India. That was nearly 18 percent of the world's total population. Many Indians live in New Delhi, the capital city. However, the country covers nearly 1.3 million square miles (3.3 million sq km). Its residents speak Hindi, English, and more than 10 other official languages.

August 15, 1947: India gains independence from the British.

October 27, 1947: The first of three wars breaks out between India and Pakistan for control of Kashmir.

January 26, 1950: India's constitution is drafted and signed into law.

January 19, 1966: Indira Gandhi becomes India's first female prime minister.

May 26, 2014: Narendra Modi becomes the prime minister of India.

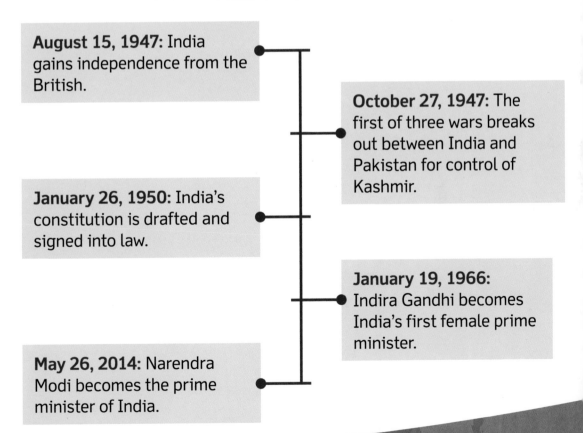

CHAPTER 3

AN EARLY ACTIVIST

The 1960s and 1970s were a time of great change in India. In 1966, Indira Gandhi became prime minister. She was the daughter of India's first prime minister, Jawaharlal Nehru. Like her father, Gandhi was a member of the Congress Party. She was the first woman to lead India's government.

Narendra Modi's life was changing, too. His parents had arranged a marriage for him in 1968.

Prime Minister Indira Gandhi gives a speech in December 1971.

But the young couple spent most of their time apart. They eventually separated, though they never divorced.

Just before Modi turned 18, he left home and began a spiritual journey. He traveled throughout India for two years. Modi studied with monks and stayed in religious retreat centers.

After his travels, Modi returned to Gujarat. He moved to Ahmedabad, the largest city in the state. During this time, India faced many problems. Drought and famine took hold of Gujarat. Oil and food prices skyrocketed.

Modi wanted to do something about these problems. So, in October 1972, he officially joined the RSS and became a pracharak. In this role, he spread the word about the group's cause. He spoke about its Hindu nationalist beliefs and worked to recruit new members. Modi worked as

▲ In 2011, Ahmedabad had a population of 5.6 million. By 2016, it had grown to more than 7 million.

an activist as well. He joined protests in Gujarat about the rising food prices.

India's government also faced problems with corruption. The Congress Party had won the 1972 elections by many votes. Gandhi's opponent accused her of **election fraud**. Three years later, a court found her guilty. The court banned Gandhi from running in another election for six years. It also removed her from Parliament.

▲ Crowds of protesters gather outside Prime Minister Gandhi's house in June 1975.

According to India's constitution, Gandhi should have stepped down as prime minister. Instead, she declared a state of emergency throughout India. Her government cracked down on people who opposed her. It **censored** the media and arrested leaders of other parties.

From 1975 to 1977, nearly 1,000 people were sent to prison for speaking out against Gandhi. Many RSS members were jailed during this time, but not Modi. He became the general secretary of Gujarat Lok Sangharsh Samiti (GLSS). This group organized protests throughout Gujarat. Modi planned secret meetings with other protest groups and helped distribute literature criticizing Gandhi's government. He even wore a disguise to pass information to imprisoned RSS leaders.

In 1977, the protesters celebrated a brief victory. Gandhi was removed from power in the general elections. But she was reelected three years later. During her 1980 campaign, she promised to fight poverty and restore law and order.

As a child, Modi had hoped to become a monk or join the Indian military. But after becoming involved with the RSS, he decided to study politics. First, he attended Delhi University. Then, in 1983, he earned a master's degree from Gujarat University. Not long after he graduated, India was in the midst of another political crisis.

CHAPTER 4

ENTERING POLITICS

For many years, relationships among India's religious groups had been tense. In 1984, that tension erupted into violence. Sikh **extremists** took over a temple in the city of Amritsar. They wanted Sikhs to have more independence. Some even called for a separate Sikh country. Prime Minister Gandhi responded by sending troops and tanks to the area in June. Hundreds of Sikhs were killed, and more than 1,500 were arrested.

Sikh extremists patrol the Golden Temple in Amritsar during the summer of 1984.

The incident set off a chain of events. First, thousands of Sikhs throughout India rioted. Then, in October, Gandhi was assassinated by two of her bodyguards, who were Sikhs. More riots broke out after her death. This time, the angry crowds attacked and killed Sikhs. Gandhi's son Rajiv took over as prime minister. But thousands more people died before he could stop the violence.

Modi continued to speak out against the Congress Party. He spent several years as a regional organizer for the RSS. In 1987, he joined the BJP, hoping to bring that party to power instead. The BJP was the political wing of the RSS. Like the RSS, the BJP promoted the view of India as a Hindu nation. It supported pro-Hindu leaders in government and education.

One of Modi's first tasks for the BJP was managing the party's campaign in Ahmedabad.

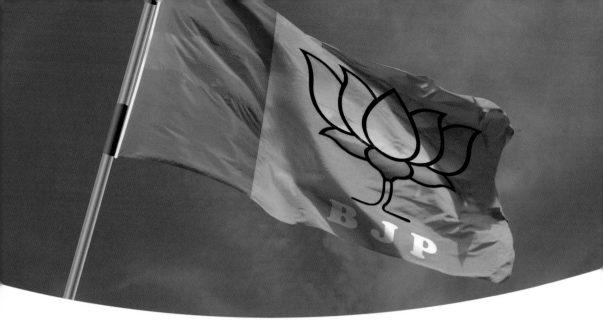

▲ The BJP is a right-wing political party with close ties to the Hindu religion.

When BJP candidates won the elections, the party promoted Modi to general secretary in Gujarat. In this role, Modi planned **rallies** across the state and raised money for the BJP. He also became the spokesperson for additional BJP campaigns.

During the next decade, Modi moved up the party's ranks. He became the national secretary of the BJP in New Delhi in 1995. He now represented the party in many states throughout India. In 1998, the BJP made Modi its national secretary.

While he was in office, fighting between religious groups broke out again. This time, the fighting centered in Kashmir. Between May and July of 1999, pro-Muslim **guerrillas** from Pakistan attacked Hindus living in Kashmir's Kargil district. India sent troops to fight back. Hundreds of

THE DISPUTED TERRITORY OF KASHMIR

AFGHANISTAN

CHINA

Shaksgam Tract: transferred from Pakistan to China but not recognized by India

Siachen Glacier: under Indian control but disputed by Pakistan

• Gilgit

Gilgit-Baltistan: under Pakistani control

Tianshuihai

Azad Kashmir: under Pakistani control

Aksai Chin: under Chinese control

• Muzaffarabad

• Kargil

• Srinagar

• Leh

PAKISTAN

• Anantnag

Jammu and Kashmir: under Indian control

New
Mirpur City

• Jammu

INDIA

people on both sides died. India and Pakistan even threatened nuclear war. A few months later, leaders from both countries attended a peace summit. They agreed not to use nuclear weapons. But their relationship remained strained.

Meanwhile, Gujarat faced problems of its own. In January 2001, an earthquake hit the city of Bhuj. Approximately 20,000 people were killed, and nearly 400,000 homes were destroyed.

In October, Modi was appointed chief minister of Gujarat. He was now the head of the state's **cabinet**. He led the state's legislature as well. Under his leadership, Bhuj was slowly rebuilt. Modi also invested in agriculture and technology. These investments, along with Modi's focus on economic development, helped Gujarat become one of the most prosperous states in India. But Modi would soon be caught up in another conflict.

CHAPTER 5

CRISIS AND CONTROVERSY

The violence began on February 27, 2002. What actually happened that day is still debated. But news outlets reported that a Muslim mob in the city of Godhra attacked a train full of Hindus. The train was returning from Ayodhya, a city in the north of India.

The attack appeared to be an act of revenge. In 1992, a group of angry Hindu nationalists had torn down a 500-year-old mosque in Ayodhya.

Fire destroyed a train in Gujarat in 2002, sparking a religious conflict across the region.

Hindus believed the mosque covered the spot where their god Ram was born. They wanted to build a temple in the mosque's place.

Passengers on the train in 2002 supposedly chanted pro-Hindu slogans. Some people believed a Muslim mob set the train on fire in response. Others said that was not the case. Whatever the cause, the fire killed 59 Hindus. Nearly 50 others were injured.

In the days following the fire, anti-Muslim riots spread throughout Gujarat. People looted stores and burned buildings. More than 1,000 people were killed. Most of the victims were Muslims.

Human rights groups accused Modi and his pro-Hindu government of ignoring the violence. Some people even suggested Modi might have had a hand in it. The BJP denied any involvement. But its members did nothing to stop the riots from

▲ Protesters call for Modi to be removed from office for failing to stop the violence.

spreading. In fact, some were later sent to jail for turning a blind eye to the attacks.

For the next 10 years, Modi continued to serve as chief minister of Gujarat. He launched building projects and improved roads in rural areas. But the riots left a dark stain on his political career.

CHAPTER 6

BECOMING PRIME MINISTER

Modi began his fourth term as chief minister of Gujarat in 2012. He had held this position longer than anyone else. And he was popular with BJP members. In fact, they chose him to lead the party in 2013. If the BJP won the 2014 election, Modi would most likely become prime minister.

For the next eight months, Modi traveled across India to raise support for the BJP. He used strategies he learned while working with the RSS.

Chief Minister Modi attends the BJP national convention in 2013.

Modi spoke at more than 400 rallies. He reached out to voters on social media as well. Modi promised to help people throughout the country, especially poor people.

When the BJP won the election, Modi became India's prime minister. Many Indians were thrilled. They hoped he would make the government less corrupt. And they were excited about his plans for the country. Modi promised to provide more jobs, education, and health care. He said he would work to help businesses earn money. Investors liked his plans to reduce federal **regulations**. They hoped the changes would boost the economy.

Other people worried about Modi's rise to power. India's Muslim citizens were especially concerned. At the time, Muslims made up approximately 14 percent of India's population. But the country had few Muslim MPs. Most MPs

△ Modi gives a speech shortly after winning the 2014 election.

who won seats in the 2014 election belonged to the BJP. With this pro-Hindu party in control, many Muslims worried the government would ignore the concerns of people who practiced other religions. They had not forgotten Modi's lack of response to the riots in 2002.

Modi was determined to prove his critics wrong. In October, he launched a program called Clean India. Among other aims, this program focused on building millions of toilets in rural areas.

As prime minister, Modi meets with leaders of other countries to discuss global issues.

Modi also organized Make in India, Digital India, and Skill India. These programs aimed to help technology companies in India grow and expand. Modi hoped they would create 100 million jobs.

In 2015, Modi began the Smart Cities Mission. This program focused on improving health and safety in cities throughout India. It helped provide housing, water, and electricity to many people.

Modi also worked to grow India's economy. During his time as prime minister, a change in national policy made investing easier. As a result, foreign countries and companies became more interested in India. Retail giants, such as IKEA and H&M, opened hundreds of stores throughout the country. Amazon and other technology companies invested in Indian businesses.

Investments from foreign countries increased as well. China promised to invest $20 billion in India's economy from 2014 to 2019. In fact, India received more than $160 billion from foreign investors between 2014 and 2017. The previous prime minister had brought in only $38 billion during his first three years.

THINK ABOUT IT ◁

What advantages does a country gain when foreign companies invest in its economy? Can you think of any disadvantages?

FOCUS ON
ARUN JAITLEY

A group called the Council of Ministers helps India's prime minister run the government. Each minister leads a different area of government. Arun Jaitley is Modi's finance minister. Jaitley is also the minister of corporate affairs. Previously, Jaitley served in Parliament. He was the leader of the BJP in the Rajya Sabha from 2009 to 2014.

Jaitley helps Modi manage the country's money. One of his main responsibilities is the government's budget. Jaitley makes plans for taxes and spending to accomplish Modi's goals.

In 2017, Jaitley devoted $710 million to helping people in rural areas find jobs. That is much more than any previous budget. Jaitley also called for tax cuts for small businesses. These businesses often failed to pay taxes. A smaller tax might persuade more businesses to pay.

▲ As finance minister, Arun Jaitley helps Modi work with Parliament to plan India's budget.

Jaitley assisted Modi with other projects as well. He made plans to build 10 million new homes for the poor. He increased spending in rural areas to build roads and give more people access to markets. Jaitley also helped Modi convince foreign countries to invest in India.

CHAPTER 7

CHALLENGES AHEAD

Modi is one of the most dynamic leaders in India's recent history. At the end of 2014, he was voted Person of the Year in *TIME*'s reader poll. However, his record in governing has been mixed.

Some of his reforms did not work as well as he had hoped. In 2016, for example, Modi issued a ban on the largest currency bills in India. He hoped to stop the flow of **counterfeit** money and prevent the government from accepting bribes.

After Modi's currency ban in 2016, many banks had a shortage of cash.

However, the ban also made it harder for people to buy and sell things. Then, in 2017, Modi began a new sales tax. Together, these two changes caused problems for the economy. Companies earned less money. Work in construction and factories slowed.

Despite Modi's programs to create jobs, unemployment throughout India has risen. Only 100,000 jobs were created in 2015, the latest year for which data is available. In comparison, an average of 579,000 jobs were added each year from 2011 to 2014.

In addition, Modi has been accused of ignoring problems, especially violence toward women and minorities. He was cleared of wrongdoing in the riots after the Godhra train fire. But his critics say that he has failed to respond to other problems. In 2015, for example, massive floods

Heavy rain in Chennai filled the city's streets with deep water and flooded thousands of homes.

wrecked the city of Chennai. Nearly 500 people died, and thousands more lost their homes. Modi's government was slow to send aid.

Another crisis occurred in January 2018. An eight-year-old Muslim girl was killed by pro-Hindu nationalists. The girl was from the state of Jammu and Kashmir. This state is part of the disputed territory along India's border. The girl's attackers wanted her Muslim community to leave this area.

They claimed to support Modi. Protests and calls for justice erupted across India. But Modi waited weeks before speaking out against the attack.

Modi faces a tough road ahead. As of 2018, the fighting in Kashmir continued. So did conflict between Hindus and Muslims in India. Many people worried that Modi's pro-Hindu leanings encouraged anti-Muslim attitudes among his followers.

Despite the criticism, Modi leads with an eye toward the future. His government set a goal to produce 175 gigawatts of renewable energy by 2022. This plan will help India fight climate

> ## THINK ABOUT IT

What recent events have sparked protests in the country where you live? What message do the protesters send to government leaders? How have the leaders responded?

△ Despite Modi's work to bring in more foreign investments, he remains a controversial figure in Indian politics.

change. India would use this energy instead of fuels such as oil and coal, which contribute to global warming. Using less of these fuels could help limit climate change. It could improve India's air quality as well.

Modi plans to help India continue to grow. In 2018, he introduced plans for reforming taxes and attracting more foreign investments. If his methods succeed, India's economy could double in size. Plans such as these keep Modi, and India, at the center of the world stage.

FOCUS ON
NARENDRA MODI

Write your answers on a separate piece of paper.

1. Write a paragraph that summarizes the main events described in Chapter 4.

2. How was Modi's first term as prime minister positive for India? How was it negative?

3. How many terms did Modi serve as the chief minister of Gujarat?

   A. two
   B. three
   C. four

4. Why was the Godhra train fire so harmful to Modi's career?

   A. It showed his lack of response to anti-Muslim feelings in the area.
   B. It was one of many examples when Modi supported pro-Muslim protesters.
   C. It showed how he took immediate action to capture troublemakers.

Answer key on page 48.

GLOSSARY

cabinet
The group of people appointed to help run the executive government of a state in India.

campaign
A series of activities such as traveling, speaking, or planning events to convince people to vote for a political candidate.

censored
Forced people not to write or publish about certain topics.

colony
An area of land that belongs to and is ruled by another country.

counterfeit
Made to look exactly like something else in order to trick people.

election fraud
The crime of interfering with an election, either by adding or taking away votes, to change the election's results.

extremists
People who hold radical political or religious views.

guerrillas
Fighters who use surprise attacks and are not part of a regular army.

inflation
A rise in prices caused by a decrease in the value of money.

rallies
Gatherings where people show support for a common cause or idea.

regulations
Rules for how a process or action must be done.

TO LEARN MORE

BOOKS

Brooks, Susie. *India.* New York: Gareth Stevens, 2017.

Marsico, Katie. *Hinduism.* Ann Arbor, MI: Cherry Lake Publishing, 2017.

Sen Gupta, Subhadra. *A Children's History of India.* New Delhi: Rupa Publications, 2015.

NOTE TO EDUCATORS

Visit **www.focusreaders.com** to find lesson plans, activities, links, and other resources related to this title.

INDEX

Ahmedabad, 18, 24

Akhil Bharatiya Vidyarthi Parishad (ABVP), 13

Amritsar, 23

Ayodhya, 29

Bharatiya Janata Party (BJP), 6, 9, 24–25, 30, 33–35, 38

Bhuj, 27

Congress Party, 5–6, 17, 19, 24

economy, 34, 36–37, 42, 45

Gandhi, Indira, 15, 17, 19–21, 23–24

Godhra, 29–30, 42

Gujarat, 11–12, 18–21, 25–27, 30–31, 33

Gujarat Lok Sangharsh Samiti (GLSS), 20

Hindu, 6, 13, 18, 24, 26, 29–30, 35, 43–44

investments, 27, 37, 39, 45

Jaitley, Arun, 38–39

Kashmir, 14–15, 26, 43–44

Muslim, 6, 13, 14, 26, 29–30, 34–35, 43–44

Pakistan, 12, 14–15, 26–27

Parliament, 8–9, 19, 38

Rashtriya Swayamsevak Sangh (RSS), 13, 18, 20–21, 24, 33

Sikh, 7, 23–24

Answer Key: 1. Answers will vary; 2. Answers will vary; 3. C; 4. A